Recipes Luce Emeriaud
Watercolours Marie-Paule Roc

The Savoy Country Cookbook

LIBRIS

I wish to thank sincerely :

- those who have generously participated in my research; especially Marcel, Nane, Arlette and Jean-François, who provided me with information and local family recipes.

- Anyone wishing to comment or obtain further information may contact me.

Luce Emeriaud

English version
© 2005 Libris
All rights reserved
ISBN 2-84799-114-X
Translation: Catherine King
Revision: Charles Akin

French version
© 2003 Libris
Tous droits réservés pour tous pays
ISBN 2-907781-18-9
2ᵉ édition avril 2004
Dépôt légal: avril 2004
Maquette: Stéphane Georis

Libris
17, rue Bayard, 38000 Grenoble
libris@libris.fr
www.libris.fr

To contact the authors:
marie-paule.roc@libertysurf.fr
luceemeriaud@hotmail.com.

Here is "The Savoy Country Cookbook" (a translation of "La cuisine des pays de Savoie"). Why this new adventure? Quite Simply because although I share my time between Grenoble—where I live—and Briançon—where I run a guesthouse, I spent my childhood in Savoy, and this region is where my roots are. I have rediscovered Savoy and my roots through this book. The mountain ranges there (the Aravis, the Bauges, the Beaufortin, the Chablais, the Mont-Blanc Massif and the Vanoise) and the valleys that lie in between (the Arve, Giffre, Maurienne and Tarentaise, among others) are quite varied and truly spectacular. As for the large local lakes— Lake Annecy, Lac du Bourget and Lake Leman, their reputation already exists. Quite naturally, this region, especially with the development of winter sports and summer and winter tourism oriented around the mountains, attracts more and more tourists and has become relatively prosperous. Mountain life has changed significantly over the past 50 years and so has local cooking. Many of the region's rural inhabitants, poor at the beginning of this century, have left their farms, although others are prospering and have contributed to the recent rediscovery of Savoy's delicious cheeses and flavoursome wines. Traditional pig raising is also still going on strongly and is providing the markets and local shops with tasty sausages, such as the famous diot, as well as with locally smoked hams and dried meats. The locals appreciate good cuisine, and a few celebrated chefs have their roots here. Mountain farmers, grocers and restaurant owners have joined forces to market the quality farm products produced in the region.

In gathering recipes and before adding my touch to them, I read the careful research of several authors, and I wish to thank them:

- Marie-Thérèse Hermann for her beautiful and well-documented work on the life of Savoy's rural inhabitants at the beginning of the twentieth century;
- Monique and Catherine Lansard, who have gathered many traditional recipes in attractive books;
- Roger Lallemand, who has described the recipes of farmers from the harsh high mountains.

It is with their help, and after many discussions with Savoyards and several short breaks in Savoy, that I was finally able to write this little cookbook. I have chosen the traditional recipes that are the tastiest and easiest to prepare. I have also included those that should not be forgotten and those that, although sometimes more complicated, are absolutely delicious. This is the case of farcement, talmouse and sabayon. I have added a few trendy recipes, such as the cheese specialties that were not part of the local peasants' diet at the beginning of last century because most of the cheese (except for the Tomme) was sold

This cookbook is, therefore, my modest contribution to the preservation of the Savoy heritage.

Marie-Paule Roc, my sister, a renowned painter of the beautiful Savoy and Dauphiné landscapes, has enlivened this book with her vibrant watercolours.

In Savoy, our ancestors, most often very poor peasants, used to consume various flour or cereal soups, which have been replaced little by little by herb or salted meat broths thickened with bread, and later made more nourishing with cheese, vegetables and sometimes a bit of bacon.

Soups

Milk and flour
soup

Serves 4 persons

. 1 quart of milk

. 2 egg yolks

. 4 slices of farmhouse bread (pain de campagne), for croutons

. 2 tablespoons of flour

. 1 tablespoon of fresh cream

. salt and pepper

This soup is quick to prepare and is rich in calcium and proteins. It is every child's favourite.

Mix the flour with half a cup of milk of milk in a bowl. Boil the remaining milk, and pour in the ingredients. Add salt and pepper.

Continue to cook for another five minutes.

Pour the resulting gruel into a large soup dish in which you have beaten two egg yolks with one tablespoon of cream.

Serve with toasted croutons.

Pasta soup

A hearty and economical soup!

Serves 4 persons

. 1.25 quarts of water

. 2 chicken stock cubes

. 2 eggs

. about 100 g of flour

. 100 g of grated Beaufort cheese

Combine the eggs, flour and a pinch of salt in a mixing bowl until you have a firm ball of dough. Roll out the dough into a thin layer (2 to 3 mm thick) on a lightly floured surface. Then, cut into small squares with a knife.

Bring the broth to the boil in a large pot, then stir in the pasta squares and cook for about 20 minutes. Serve with grated cheese.

Soup
with greens

In Savoy and the Dauphiné, farmers prepare this poor man's soup with greens (*herbes*) from the garden. The greens are various leaved vegetables, namely celery, lamb's lettuce (*mâche*), sorrel (*oseille*), chervil (*cerfeuil*) and wild comestible greens—dandelion (*pissenlit*), plantain, wild lamb's lettuce and, of course, nettles.

Serves 4 persons

. a large bunch of greens
. 1.25 quarts of lightly salted water
. 4 medium-sized potatoes
. butter or fresh cream

Cook the pealed potatoes cut into small pieces in salted water in a large stew pot. While they are cooking, wash the greens and chop them fine. When the potatoes are cooked, mix the potatoes and broth in a blender and add the chopped greens. Return this to the stew pot and continue cooking for several minutes. Serve with fresh cream or butter.

Nettle *soup*

Serves 4 persons

· a large bunch of nettles, shoots
  or the tender tips
· 1.5 quarts of salted water
· 2 tablespoons of fresh cream
· 2 good-sized slices of toasted farmhouse bread
· 2 garlic cloves, crushed
· salt and pepper

*Stinging-
nettle soup is
greatly appreciated
in Savoy, especially in
the spring when young nettle
leaves can be found. Nevertheless, it
is still possible to prepare this soup at the beginning of summer by
using tender branches that have not yet flowered.*

After washing and draining the nettle leaves, brown
them in olive oil or butter in a large pot. Add the
pealed potatoes cut into pieces, and cover with
salted water. Bring to the boil and cook for 20
minutes. Then mix this in a blender. Add the
fresh cream just before serving.
        Serve separately the croutons rubbed
with garlic.

Onion soup
au gratin

Serves 4 persons

- 2 large onions
- 1.25 quarts of beef stock
  (or water and two bouillon cubes)
- 2 tablespoons of flour
- 1 glass of white wine from Savoy
- 4 slices of toasted farmhouse bread (pain de campagne)
- grated cheese (Gruyere or Beaufort)

In a large cast-iron pot, brown the sliced onions in a mixture of oil and butter. When they begin to brown, sprinkle them with two tablespoons of flour. Mix with a wooden spoon until the flour turns slightly brown.

Cover with the bouillon and white wine and continue cooking for 15 minutes while stirring.

To serve, pour the soup into an open ovenproof soup tureen, place the toasted bread on top of the soup, sprinkle with the grated cheese and place the tureen under the oven grill until the bread and cheese become golden.

Sorrel soup

Serves 6 persons

. 2 large handfuls of sorrel
. 3 slices of stale farmhouse bread (pain de campagne)
. oil or butter

   Brown the washed and trimmed
sorrel and the bread cut into small
pieces in cooking oil or butter in a
large saucepan.
   Add two quarts of salted water and
cook for half an hour. Mix this in a blender
and serve with a small ladleful of fresh cream.

A hearty soup

Serves 6 to 8 persons

. 2 or 3 leeks

. 4 or 5 carrots

. 3 or 4 turnips

. 1 branch of celery

. 1/2 a green cabbage

. 1 potato per person

. 400 g of smoked bacon

. 1 large raw sausage
  (Pormonaise or Longeole in Savoy)

. 1 or 2 pig's feet
  (optional, but advisable)

Hearty, because the salted pork is cooked in the soup with the vegetables. This soup is a nutritious main dish.

Brown the vegetables peeled and cut into small pieces (except the potatoes) in a large stew pot in the olive oil for several minutes. Cover with 2.5 quarts of lightly salted water (the lard is already very salty) and bring to the boil. Add the meat and cook for one hour.

Remove the meat and set it aside in a warm place.

Serve the vegetable soup with thin slices of farmhouse bread (pain de campagne) and thin slices of Tomme cheese.

Then, serve the meat with the boiled potatoes.

Savoy squash
soup

For 6 persons

. 1.2 kg of squash
. 1 quart of milk
. 50 g of butter
. 2 garlic cloves, chopped
. 100 g of grated Gruyere cheese
. salt and pepper

This classic soup made its way to many countries in the world from France where it began as a satisfying hot soup among the country folk. Here is the original recipe from Savoy.

Peel and dice the squash. Combine the squash, chopped garlic, one-half cup of water, salt and pepper in a covered saucepan and braise for 20 minutes. Mash the mixture with a vegetable press and pour in the boiling milk. Boil for another 10 minutes.

Serve with the grated cheese and croutons.

Chestnut soup

This is another 'heavy' soup for winter. This recipe came from close by in Valle d'Aosta, brought to Savoy by a peddler or traveller. Not all Savoyards have chestnut trees, but they brought a supply of chestnuts at the autumn produce markets

For 6 to 8 persons

. 1 handful of chestnuts per person
. 1 handful of rice per person
. 1 or 2 raw sausages
  (a Longeole is quite suitable)
. 1.5 quarts of water
. 1 quart of milk

Slit the chestnuts and soak them for five minutes in boiling water. Drain and peel them. Bring the water and milk to the boil. Add salt and slowly pour in the rice and chestnuts. Add the sausages and let them cook a good half hour.
Slice the sausages, mash the chestnuts in a vegetable press, put the sausages in the soup and serve.

Wild garlic soup

You can find wild garlic, a cousin of the domesticated garlic, in the spring in the humid undergrowth. Its leaves resemble those of the lily of the valley, and its star-shaped flowers have a very strong smell of garlic, which makes it easy to recognize. To prepare this soup, simply use the recipe for nettle soup, replacing the nettles with wild garlic leaves and flowers. This soup is delicious and healthful. Wild garlic improves digestion, lowers blood pressure and is effective against the cough and common cold.

15

All the simple vegetables are used in the Savoyard kitchen: Swiss chard, celery, leeks, broad beans, cabbage, carrots, spinach, and above all turnips, which used to be the most common vegetable eaten in the mountains. The cardoon is often reserved for the holidays at the end of the year. Today, mixed salads are in fashion, and everyone can be inventive, combining ingredients to their taste. Long ago, the need to prepare meals quickly and the seasons dictated simple salads.

Salads *and* vegetables

Potato salad

Serves 6 persons

. 1 kg of potatoes
. 1 cup dry white wine
. shallots, parsley and caraway seeds
. a well-seasoned red-wine vinaigrette

Caraway seeds (carvi) from a wild plant easily found in mountain fields greatly add to this simple dish

Cook the washed
but unpeeled potatoes
in salted water. Peel
them and slice them
while still warm into a
salad bowl. Add salt
and pepper. Sprinkle with
the white wine. Keep warm.
Pour on the vinaigrette just before serving.
Sprinkle with the chopped parsley and shallots and
the caraway seeds.

This salad is an excellent accompaniment for a warm sausage (Longeole)
poached for 30 minutes in boiling water.

Dandelion salad

Serves 6 persons

. 300 g of dandelion leaves
. 6 hard or soft-boiled eggs
. 3 garlic cloves
. a well-seasoned vinaigrette
. toasted croutons rubbed with garlic

What could be better than these young and tender dandelions that sprout from the ground at the first signs of melting snow?

Preparing dandelions is time consuming; I prefer to clean them where I pick them and as I go along. On a sunny day, it is a real pleasure.

Wash the dandelions several times. Pat dry and place them in a salad bowl.

Prepare croutons by rubbing several slices of toasted bread with garlic and then cutting the bread into small cubes.

Boil the eggs and peel them.

Sprinkle the salad with the vinaigrette and add two chopped garlic cloves. Toss well.

Add the croutons and the hard-boiled eggs cut in two or whole if they are soft-boiled.

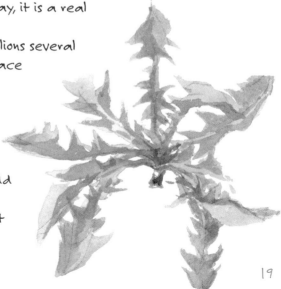

Spinach omelette

Serves 6 persons

. 6 to 8 eggs
. 500 g of spinach
. 2 leeks (the white part only)
. a bunch of chervil

Finely chop the washed spinach, leeks and chervil.
Brown them in a frying pan with butter and oil and
season to taste.
Then pour in the beaten eggs, adding salt and pepper to
taste. Continue cooking until the omelette has set.
Serve with a warm thick tomato sauce.

Spinach bread

Serves 6 persons

. 1 kg of spinach

. 200 g of Tomme cheese

. 9 eggs

. salt, pepper, curry powder

Cook the spinach for several minutes in salted boiling water and then drain well. Finely chop the Tomme. Separate the yolks from the egg whites. Beat the yolks with the spices, and then beat the egg white until stiff. Mix the spinach with the yolks and carefully pour in the egg white. Place this preparation in a buttered cake pan and cook in the oven for 35 minutes at a temperature of 180° C. This can be eaten either warm or cold and is best accompanied with a fresh tomato sauce.

Swiss chard gratin

Serves 4 persons

. 1.5 kg of Swiss chard (blettes)

. 100 g of Beaufort cheese

. 30 g of butter

. 1 heaping tablespoon of flour

. 100g of fresh cream

Cut off the green part of the Swiss chard and keep it for the following recipe, the farcette.

Thin out the midribs if necessary, and cut into small pieces. Cook in boiling salted water for 20 minutes.

Meanwhile, make a white roux with the butter, flour and a ladleful of cooking stock. Season to taste and add the grated cheese and fresh cream.

Drain the Swiss chard well, pour on the roux, and place this in a gratin dish. Cook for 10 minutes in a hot oven (200° C).

Baked cabbage
parcels

This speciality prepared everywhere in Savoy, from the Arve Valley to the Combe de Savoie.

Serves 4 persons

. 16 Swiss chard leaves
. 200 g of bacon
. 1 cooking sausage
. 3 handfuls of sultanas
. 2 eggs
. 1 carrot
. f1 leek
. flour, pepper, nutmeg
. grated cheese

Wash the Swiss chard leaves and set aside four large leaves.

Cook the others in boiling salted water for 5 to 10 minutes. Drain them, chop them finely, and then place them in a salad bowl with the sultanas, eggs and enough flour to making a stuffing that is consistent.

Then, cook the bacon and sausage in boiling water, with a bouquet garni, several leek leaves and the carrot for 30 minutes.

Split the Swiss chard leaves that were set aside. In each half leaf, place a handful of farce and make a parcel. Place the parcels in an oven dish. Sprinkle with grated cheese and several knobs of butter. Pour in the pork bouillon and bake for 20 minutes in a hot oven.

Serve the farcettes warm, accompanied with the warm bacon and sausage.

Cardoon *gratin*

Serves 6 persons

. 1.5 kg of cardoon

. 150 g of Gruyere

. 3 tablespoons of beef stock

. 50 g of butter

. 2 tablespoons of flour

Carefully peel the cardoon and remove any dark or hard branches and the leaves. Wash the stems, then remove the white skin and pull off the large strings. Cut them into small pieces.

Cook in salted boiling water for 1.25 hours until the cardoon is tender. Drain and set aside the bouillon. Make a roux with the flour, butter (or oil) and two ladlefuls of cooking stock. Add the grated Gruyere cheese.

Place the drained cardoons mixed with the roux in a gratin dish and bake in a hot oven for 20 minutes.

Note: You can cook a bone with marrow with the cardoon and place the marrow, cut into slices, on the gratin 10 minutes before the end of the cooking.

Cabbage *with chestnuts*

. 1 large cabbage

. 300 g of bacon

. 500 g of peeled chestnuts

Remove the core and cut the cabbage into eight pieces. Cook this in salted boiling water with the bacon.

Cook the peeled chestnuts separately.

Drain the cabbage, bacon and chestnuts. Brown them in a pan with a bit of butter or oil after having diced the bacon.

Note: This dish can also be prepared as a gratin by alternating layers of cabbage and chestnuts with a bit of grated cheese and a touch of flour. Add the cheese and moisten with bouillon or milk. In this case, don't add the bacon. Bake it in a hot oven for 15 minutes.

La Chenal, a hamlet above Bozel

Savoyard leeks

Serves 6 persons
. 1.5 kg of leeks
. 150 g of grated cheese
. breadcrumbs
. grated nutmeg
. fresh cream

Cut the well cleaned
leeks into 5-centimetre-long
pieces. Cook them in salted boiling
water and then drain well.

Place them in an open ovenproof dish.
Sprinkle with breadcrumbs, grated cheese and
the nutmeg and then repeat with another layer.

Pour on some fresh cream.

Bake for half an hour in a hot oven (180 to 200° C).

"Mange-tout"
or sweet peas

Serves 4 persons
. 1 kg of snow peas
. 1 slice of bacon
. 1 large white onion
. a few leaves of lettuce

Dice the bacon.

In a frying pan, lightly brown the bacon with the chopped onion and a bit of oil or butter.

Add the sweet peas and lettuce leaves. Braise them by placing a lid on the frying pan for 30 to 40 minutes.

Serve right away.

Turnips

Turnips are those round, hard, white and purple vegetables that should not be confused with the long and white navettes. Turnips composed a large share of the food of the eighteenth-century peasants living in isolated mountainous areas; to the point that the local inhabitants were called "ravichets" or "pica ravas". Here are two easy recipes for preparing them.

Buttered turnips

Serves 4 to 5 persons
. 1 kg of turnips
. butter and oil
. salt, pepper

In a large frying pan (or wok), heat up a little butter and oil and fry the washed and diced turnips until golden. Cover with a lid and cook for another 15 minutes. Season to taste.

Serve with grilled sausages.

Turnips "en gratin"

Serves 4 to 6 persons
. 1 kg of radishes
. 500 g of peeled and cooked chestnuts
. 50 g of butter
. 50 g of flour
. 150 g of grated Beaufort cheese
. salt and pepper

Cook the diced turnips in salted boiling water for 15 to 20 minutes. Drain, combine with the chestnuts and arrange in an ovenproof dish.

Prepare a béchamel sauce by briefly heating the flour combined with butter, add some milk, bring to the boil and stir for a further two minutes. Season to taste. Add the grated Beaufort cheese. Pour this sauce on the vegetables. Bake the dish in a hot oven for about 15 minutes.

This gratin is best served with a pork roast.

Salted épogne

Serves 6 to 8 persons

. 1 cup of lukewarm milk
. 1.5 teaspoons of active dry yeast
. 300 g of flour
. 2 eggs
. salt, a few saffron threads

The épogne, half way between bread and brioche, is a specialty of the Bauges and Combe de Savoie.

Dissolve the yeast and warm milk in a bowl and set aside for 15 minutes. The mixture will start to foam, indicating that the yeast is active. In another bowl, combine well the flour, salt, saffron threads, eggs, and then add the milk and yeast.

Knead this mixture into a thick ball of dough and set aside for three hours in a warm and damp place.

Knead again and roll out into a greased pie tin or baking tin. Bake for one hour in a hot oven (180 to 200° C).

Epogne *with vegetables*

Epogne with pumpkin

Arrange 800 g of diced raw pumpkin on the dough.
Combine 150 g of fresh cream, 2 eggs, 150 g of cream, 150 g of grated cheese, salt and pepper.
Pour this mixture over the pumpkin.
Bake in a hot oven (180 to 200° C) for one hour.

Epogne with spinach

Follow the above recipe but replace the pumpkin with chopped cooked spinach.

31

Carrots Val de Thônes

Serves 4 persons

. 6 large carrots
. a handful of sultanas
. 100 g of diced bacon
. 30 g of butter and 1 tablespoon of oil
. 1 tablespoon of flour

This is an excellent original recipe for this very common vegetable.

Dice the peeled carrots.
Brown the carrots with the bacon
in butter and oil.
Sprinkle with the flour, add the sultanas, cover with a lid and
continue simmering for half an hour.

Pumpkin
gratin

Serves 6 persons

. 1.5 kg of pumpkin
. 200 g of thick fresh cream
. 150 g of grated Beaufort cheese
. 3 garlic cloves
. 1 bouquet garni
. salt, pepper, nutmeg, cayenne pepper

Cook the peeled pumpkin without its seeds in salted boiling water with the bouquet garni and garlic for 15 minutes.

Drain well. Rub a baking dish with the garlic and pour in the diced pumpkin.

Add grated nutmeg, some pepper, a dash of cayenne pepper and cover with the cream. Mix carefully and sprinkle with the grated cheese.

Bake for 15 to 20 minutes (180° C) or until golden but still moist.

In Savoy, potatoes are called "tartifle", "truffe" or "trifle".
Mountain potatoes are delicious, and there are hundreds of
recipes for preparing them.

Potato, polenta and *pasta dishes*

"Fricassée"

Serves 6 persons

. 1 kg of potatoes
  (Charlotte ou bintje)

. 2 to 4 onions

. butter, drippings or a mixture
  of butter and oil

. salt, pepper

In Savoy, this is the most common recipe used for preparing potatoes. It is especially delicious if good-quality ingredients are used.

In a heavy frying pan (or wok), heat the
butter and oil mixture or the drippings, and lightly
fry the thinly sliced onions until they turn golden.
Stir in the sliced potatoes and cook until golden, while
turning from time to time with a wooden spoon.
Add salt and pepper.
After cooking, lower the heat and cover until ready to serve.

"Fricassée"
with Reblochon cheese

Serves 4 persons

. 1 kg of potatoes

. 2 or 3 onions

. 1 Reblochon cheese

. mixture of butter and oil

. salt, pepper

This recipe originated in the Aravis region, where the Reblochon, an excellent round and pink creamy cheese, is produced. Alternatively, a washed-rind cheese can be used instead of a Reblochon cheese.

Prepare a "fricassée" with the onions and potatoes.

Scrape the crust of the Reblochon, and then cover the onions and potatoes with the two halves of the Reblochon split in to.

Continue cooking until the Reblochon melts into the potatoes.

Serve with a green salad.

Note: If you add diced bacon to this, you have a tartiflette

"Paillasson" potatoes

Serves 6 persons

. 1 kg of grated potatoes

. 150 g of grated onions

. 2 eggs

. 1 tablespoon of flour

. parsley, nutmeg, chives

. peanut oil

Toss all the ingredients with the chopped herbs in a large bowl.

Heat the peanut oil in a heavy frying pan and when the oil has heated fry spoonfuls of this mixture on both sides until crisp and golden.

Drain on absorbent paper.

This dish was traditionally served on Fridays accompanied by a green salad.

"Ravioles"
from the Chablais region

Serves 6 persons

. 1 kg of potatoes

. 2 eggs

. flour

. chopped garlic, chives and chervil

. salt, pepper

Steam the unpeeled potatoes until tender. Peel them and then mash them until very smooth, adding the eggs, herbs, salt and pepper (you can add extra flavour with grated cheese).

Allow to this mixture to cool, and then add just enough flour to be able to form small balls that can be rolled out as quenelles.

Set these quenelles aside to cool for one hour, and then fry them in boiling oil.

Heat about one inch of oil in a frying pan.

Fry the balls, turning constantly with two spoons until crisp and brown all over.

Each village has its own recipe for ravioli.

Scalloped potatoes

Serves 6 persons

. 1 kg of potatoes
. 300 g of cheese
. beef stock
. butter
. salt, pepper, garlic

Alternate layers of sliced potatoes and grated cheese in a well-buttered gratin dish.

Sprinkle each layer with chopped garlic, salt and pepper.

Top with a layer of grated cheese.

Cover with the beef stock and add a few knobs of butter.

Bake in a medium oven (160 to 180° C) for one hour.

"Farcon" from Faucigny

Serves 6 persons

. 1.5 kg of potatoes
. 2 apples
. 4 onions
. 3 eggs
. 150 g of sultanas
. 0.5 quart of milk
. 75 g of butter
. 150 g of grated cheese
. salt and pepper

"Farcon" and "farcement" are typical Savoyard dishes using potatoes and dried fruits. They were usually prepared on Saturday evening and cooked slowly over very low heat until Sunday morning to be ready to eat for lunch right after Mass.

Here is one recipe from among many. Soak the sultanas in the warm milk for one hour. Boil the potatoes, then peel and mash them.
Add the milk and the beaten eggs and mix well. Stir in the sliced apples, sultanas and grated cheese. Add the sliced and browned onions. Pour this into a buttered ovenproof dish.
Add some butter and bake in a hot oven (200° C) for half an hour until the farçon has puffed and browned.
Accompany this dish with a green salad.

"Farcement"

Serves 6 to 8 persons

. 1.5 kg of potatoes
. 350 g of pitted prunes
. 250 g of sultanas
. 200 g of dried or fresh pears
. 250 g of diced bacon
. 30 thin slices of smoked bacon
. 2 eggs
. 50 g of melted butter
. salt, pepper, nutmeg
. some saffron threads, a dash of cinnamon
. 1/2 cup of local eau de vie

A rich dish that used to take pride of place on Savoy tables on Sundays and special occasions. Every village had its own recipe. It is generally baked in a "rabolire" mould, but a "kugelhopf" baking tin works as well. This is a delicious dish well worth its time-consuming preparation.

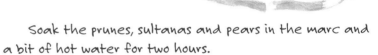

Soak the prunes, sultanas and pears in the marc and a bit of hot water for two hours.

Grate the potatoes in a large bowl and add all the ingredients. Season to taste.

Line the mould with the slices of bacon, then pour in the mixture. Top with a few slices of bacon.

Cover with a lid or aluminium foil. Place this mould in a baking tin with about two inches of cold water.

Bake for two to three hours in a slow oven (150° C) and serve sliced with boiled or grilled sausages.

Cabbage "farcement"

Serves 6 persons

. 1 large cabbage
. 1 kg of potatoes
. 150 g of prunes
. 2 handfuls of sultanas
. 150 g of diced bacon
. 1 sliced onion
. 2 tablespoons of sugar
. salt
. 1 egg
. 1 tablespoon of flour
. milk
. 50 g butter

Soak sultanas and prunes in warm water for one hour. Boil the cabbage for 10 to 15 minutes.

Drain well and then place it on a large round dish in which four long strings are crossed in the centre. Delicately open the leaves and remove the core of the cabbage.

Steam the potatoes, then peel and mash them until smooth.

Combine the mashed potatoes with the other ingredients, including the chopped cabbage core and the browned chopped onion.

Stuff the cabbage with this preparation, alternating cabbage and stuffing and wrap tightly with the strings.

Place the cabbage in a greased heavy saucepan, add two cups of beef stock and bake in a slow oven for four hours.

Cover with a lid after a couple of hours. If necessary, add a little water to the pan to prevent scorching.

Polenta

Serves 6 persons

. 250 g of pre-cooked polenta

. 50 g butter

. 150 g of grated Beaufort cheese

Polenta is fine maize semolina that originated in the Italian Piedmont region. Almost all Savoyards love to eat polenta. It is delicious accompanied with casseroles and diots (Savoy sausages). You can now buy pre-cooked polenta, although food lovers often prefer the non-pre-cooked polenta.

Pour the polenta into one quart of salted boiling water. Stir constantly while cooking for 5 to 6 minutes.

The polenta thickens quickly. Continue cooking and stirring until a wooden spoon can stand by itself.

Serve the polenta as it is with butter and grated Beaufort cheese as an accompaniment for meat and gravy.

Polenta gnocchi

Prepare the polenta as indicated in the previous recipe. Spread it on a greased baking sheet to a thickness of about half of an inch. Let it cool and then cut it into small two-inch squares. Arrange those squares in an ovenproof dish, and then sprinkle them with grated cheese and knobs of butter.

Bake for 15 minutes in a hot oven (200° C). Serve with a tomato sauce seasoned with herbes de Provence, olive oil and garlic.

Deep fried polenta

Deep fry the polenta squares (see above recipe) until crispy and golden.

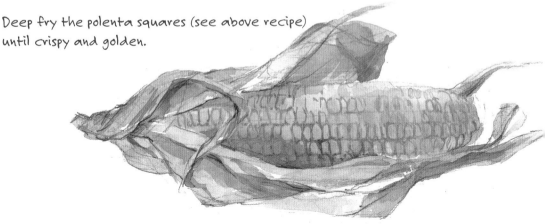

Polenta "farcement"

Serves 6 persons

. 250 g of pre-cooked polenta

. 50 g of butter

. 150 g of grated Beaufort cheese

. 50 g of sultanas

. 300 g of prunes
  (soaked in lukewarm water)

. 200 g of diced bacon

. nutmeg

Pour the polenta into one quart of salted boiling water. Add the sultanas, prunes and diced bacon and stir constantly for five to six minutes.

Then add the butter, cheese and a pinch of nutmeg. Mix well and pour the preparation into a buttered mould. Keep warm.

To serve, cut into slices on a serving plate.

This is best eaten with diots and Longeoles (grilled or boiled thick pork sausages).

Crozets

Crozets are tiny pasta squares made with wheat and buckwheat flour, eggs, salt and pepper

Home-made crozets

Combine 300 g of wheat flour, 200 g of buckwheat flour, 2 eggs, salt and pepper. Add lukewarm water and knead the dough well until smooth and firm. Then roll out the dough to a thickness of about 1/10 of an inch. Let it rest for one hour.

Cut the dough into long thin ribbons, and then cut the ribbons into small squares. You need only 20 minutes to cook fresh crozets.

Ready-to-cook crozets

Serves 6 persons
. 300 g of ready-to-cook crozets
. fresh cream or sarfuze
. grated Beaufort cheese
. salt and pepper

Packaged ready-to-cook crozets are available from most food stores.

Cook the crozets in a large amount of boiling water or chicken stock for at least 40 minutes. Drain and pour into an ovenproof dish. Cover with grated cheese and fresh cream and bake in a hot oven for 15 minutes.

Alternatively, cover the crozets with grated cheese and sarfuze and serve right away.

You can prepare sarfuze by lightly browning chopped onions, chopped garlic and diced bacon with butter in a pan.

Cooking
"fides" style

This is a time-honoured way to cook rice and pasta in Savoy

Brown a chopped onion in butter, and add the pasta or rice. Continue to cook for several minutes and slowly add salted boiling water.

Continue cooking until the pasta or rice has swollen and no longer absorbs water.

This cooking method is directly inspired by the Italian way to prepare risotto. It is a very delicious way of preparing rice or pasta.

Typically, fresh meat did not often grace the tables of the poor Savoy farmers. Pork, but also goat and more rarely beef, used to be salted and stored for the whole year. As a consequence, the Savoy region is well known for cooked, smoked and dried hams and many varieties of sausages such as diots, Longeoles, Parmoniers or Pormonaises.

Meat dishes

One can still taste the wonderful traditional recipes of bourgeois households in many of the region's restaurants

Notre-Dame-de-Bellecombe

Diots

Diots are thick pork sausages that can be prepared in several ways. They used to be grilled on a grapevine shoots in the middle of the vineyards

Diots in white wine

Serves 4 persons

. 8 diots

. 2 to 3 potatoes per person

. 1 bottle of dry white wine from Savoy

. several grapevine shoots

Put the unpeeled potatoes in a heavy saucepan. Cover them with the grapevine shoots arranged in a grid. Pour in the white wine. Add the diots pricked with a fork on top of the grapevine shoots. Cover and bring to the boil. Cook for one hour. The diots will cook in the wine vapour and their fat will drip on the potatoes below. Serve with Dijon mustard and fresh butter.

Beaufort Diots

Serves 4 persons

. 8 diots

. 2 to 3 peeled and crushed tomatoes

. 1/2 bottle of dry white wine from Savoy

. 2 shallots and 1 onion, sliced

. 1 tablespoon of flour

Lightly brown the diots in peanut oil until golden. Set them aside in a warm place. Briefly simmer the onion and the shallots the frying pan. Sprinkle with the flour and add the white wine. Season to taste. Stir with a wooden spoon until this sauce is smooth. Add the tomatoes and the diots. Simmer for half an ho Serve with steamed potatoes.

Other sausages
and how to cook them

Magland sausages
These small pork sausages are prepared with the meat that is left on the bones once all the main meat cuts have been removed. They are seasoned with salt and pepper and then preserved in oil. You can cook them just like the diots.

Longeoles (from the lower Arve valley and the Chablais region)
These sausages are prepared with pork and lots of lard and are flavoured with salt, pepper and cumin.
They are delicious cooked in boiling water for about 20 minutes with potatoes.

Pormonaises
These sausages are made with minced pork offal combined with cooked and chopped cabbage, then smoked. They are best cooked like the Longeoles.

Pormoniers
These pork-neck sausages are seasoned with Swiss chard leaves, chopped leek, salt and pepper.
You can lightly grill or boil them.

The hamlet of Boudin

"Potée"
savoyarde

Serves 6 persons

. 1 slightly salted pork shank
. 500 g of slightly salted pork ribs
. 6 diots and 1 or 2 Longeoles
. 300 g of smoked pork belly
. 1 large cabbage
. 6 carrots
. 6 turnips
. 12 potatoes
. 1 onion
. cloves, pepper, thyme, bay leaf
. c and juniper berries berries

Cook the meat in a large pot with the carrots, turnips and the herbs, but without the sausages. Pick the onion with the cloves and add this to the pot.

Peel the cabbage and cut it into 6 pieces, then blanch them for five minutes.

Peel the potatoes. When the meat and vegetables have cooked for about an hour and a half, add the cabbage, potatoes and sausages. Continue cooking for another 45 minutes.

Serve the meat cut into pieces on a large plate and the vegetables on another, accompanied with Dijon mustard.

54

Stuffed cabbage

This is a delicious dish that is easy to prepare with meat leftovers

Serves 6 persons

. 1 large cabbage
. 500 to 600 g of meat leftovers or cold cuts
. 2 slices of farmhouse bread (pain de campagne)
. 1 large onion, 1 shallot
. some parsley
. 2 garlic cloves
. 1 egg
. 1 salt and pepper

Mince the meat, bread, onion, shallot, garlic and parsley. Add the egg and season to taste.

Put the cabbage in a large pot of salted boiling water and cook for 15 minutes, then drain it upside down in a colander.

Arrange four strings to form a cross in a round dish. Place the cabbage on the strings and open the leaves carefully. Remove the core and replace it with a handful of the stuffing. Fold back the leaves one by one, placing stuffing between the leaves. Close the cabbage and tie the strings tightly.

Heat 50 g of duck fat or lard in a heavy saucepan or pressure cooker, and brown the cabbage on all sides. Add a large cup of beef stock and cover with a lid.

Simmer for almost two hours on a slow fire. Check frequently that there is enough liquid to prevent scorching and add water, if necessary.

Attriaux and "Fricassée"

Both these recipe are prepared with pork offal (heart, liver, kidney and sometimes even the lungs).

Attriaux

To prepare the attriaux, use equal parts of chopped pork liver, heart and kidneys that have been with chopped leeks, shallots and onions, salt, pepper and nutmeg. Rap small balls of this mince in pieces of caul (crépine) and flatten them. That gives patties should be cooked in a frying pan for about ten minutes.

"Fricassée"

Dice pork heart, liver and kidney (and lung if you like), then brown them in a bit of oil. Coat with flour. Add some diluted red wine. Season with salt, pepper, bay leaf and thyme and simmer for half an hour.

Pork paupiettes
with Reblochon cheese

Serves 6 persons

. 12 thin slices of pork fillet

. 1 Reblochon cheese

. 500 g of prunes

. 2 tablespoons of peanut oil

. 1/2 cup of marc de Savoy or Cognac

. 300 ml of chicken stock

. thyme, bay leaf, salt and pepper

This is a very tasty recipe that uses three products from Savoy: pork, Reblochon cheese and dried prunes.

Scrape the crust of the Reblochon and cut it into thin slices. Put one or two slices of Reblochon on each slice of pork fillet plus two juicy pitted prunes. Make parcels by rolling the pieces on themselves (paupiette) and tie each with string.

Heat the oil in an anti-adhesive frying pan, and brown the parcels on all sides. Salt and pepper. Sprinkle with the Cognac or marc and light. Pour on the bouillon.

Add the thyme and the bay leaf and cover to simmer for 25 minutes. Add the remaining prunes during the cooking. Set the parcels aside on a warm plate. Add the cream into the pan juices. Thicken this gravy, and pour it on the parcels or serve it separately.

Pork casserole
with red wine and cream

Serves 5 to 6 persons

. 1 kg of pork fillet

. 3/4 bottle of red wine

. 2 onions

. 2 tablespoons of local eau de vie or Cognac

. 1 tablespoon of flour

. 50 g of fresh cream

. salt, pepper, bay leaf and thyme

Cut the fillet into large two-inch cubes. Marinate them in red wine with sliced onions, the thyme, bay leaf and a bit of olive oil for at least 12 hours.

Then drain the meat and pat it dry. Brown it in an enamelled cast iron pan with a bit of oil or better some lard. Season to taste with salt and pepper. Sprinkle with flour, stir and then pour on the marinade. Bring to a boil, and let simmer for one hour or until the meat is tender.

Add the Cognac and fresh cream, and continue cooking for another 15 minutes with the lid slightly ajar in order for the sauce to reduce and thicken. Serve with polenta and grated cheese.

Note: This dish is even better when prepared with pork filet mignon, and the cooking time is a bit less.

Braised veal with fresh cream

Serves 4 persons

. 1 kg of veal breast,
  cut into small cubes

. 250 g of button mushrooms

. 1 or 2 stock cubes

. 1 egg yolk

. vegetable oil or butter

. 100 g of fresh cream

. ljuice from half a lemon

. garlic, thyme and laurel

. salt and pepper

Brown the cubes of veal in an enamelled cast-iron saucepan with two tablespoons of cooking oil (or 30 g of butter). Salt and pepper. Sprinkle with flour and cover with the bouillon. Add the thyme, bay leaf and garlic. Let simmer for one hour.

In the meantime, cook the thinly sliced mushrooms separately in a frying pan with one tablespoon of water, 25 g of butter, the juice of half a lemon, a pinch of salt and a pinch of sugar.

To serve, put the pieces of meat on a warm plate and thicken the sauce with the egg yolk, cream and mushrooms. Heat without boiling until the sauce thickens. Pour it on the meat and serve.

Note: You can prepare this same recipe with pieces of chicken.

Braised beef
with white wine
and mushroom sauce

Serves 8 persons

. 1.5 kg of beef shoulder cut into small cubes
. 150 g of smoked bacon
. 1/2 bottle of dry white wine
. 1/2 quart of water
. 3 large onions, chopped
. 1 large clove-studded onion
. 3 celery branches
. 3 or 4 carrots
. a bouquet garni
. 3 garlic cloves
. 250 g of button mushrooms

In an enamelled cast-iron pot, lightly brown the diced bacon. Set that aside before it browns. In the same pan, add the meat and brown it on all the sides. Add the onions; cover and braise for two minutes, then add the chopped carrots and celery. Pour in the white wine and the water; add the bouquet garni, the garlic, onion and clove and the bacon. Season with salt and pepper. Cover and let simmer for two hours. Add the mushrooms cut into quarters, and continue cooking for another hour.

Chambéry Beef Aiguillette

Serves 8 persons

- 1.5 kg of aiguillette,
  larded with thin slices of smoked bacon
- 1 bottle of red wine
- 2 large onions, sliced
- 2 carrots
- 2 or 3 garlic cloves
- tomato paste
- thyme, bay leaf, salt and pepper

Brown the meat on all sides in a bit of oil or lard. Add salt, pepper and the chopped carrots and onions. Sprinkle with flour and add enough red wine to cover half the meat.

Add the thyme, bay leaf, crushed garlic and one tablespoon of tomato paste. Let simmer for about two and a half hours, turning the meet from time to time during cooking. This cut of meat is very tender and flavoursome when cooked this way and is best served with polenta.

63

Pullet with Beaufort cheese

This recipe is from Philippe Million and was published in "Cuisine du terroir".

Serves 6 persons

. 1 fat pullet (*young hen*) (*about 2 kg*)
. 100 g of butter
. 100 g of fresh cream
. 150 of Beaufort cheese
. 50 g of flour

Prepare a good bouillon with the chicken giblets, a clove-studded onion, a branch of celery, thyme, bay leaf, parsley, two garlic cloves, four carrots, salt and pepper. Bring to a boil and cook the chicken for one hour.

Remove it from the pot and carve it up, setting aside the pieces in a warm place. Put the carcass back into the bouillon and cook until the bouillon is reduced by half. Strain it.

Prepare a white roux with the butter, flour and bouillon. Add the cream and continue cooking for a few seconds.

Remove from the heat and add the Beaufort cut in slices. Place the pieces of pieces of chicken in a baking dish, cover with the sauce and brown under the grill.

Philippe Million recommends serving this dish with cooked Jerusalem artichokes (topinambours).

Chambéry veal paté

*This is a traditional recipe from
the Combe de Savoie.*

Serves 6 persons

. 750 g of veal roast
. 1/2 a cup of vinegar
. 100 g of bacon, diced
. 1 onion
. several branches of parsley
. 100 g of pickled lemon
. 1 cup of water

For the pastry:

. 400 g of flour
. 130 g of butter
. 70 g of lard
. 3 egg yolks, salt

For the sauce:

. 50 g of butter
. 2 tablespoons of flour
. 1/4 quart of broth (or beef stock)
. 1 tablespoon of vinegar
. 2 tablespoons of Madera wine
. salt and pepper

Marinate the meat cut into small cubes overnight in the water and vinegar. Mix the flour, salt, butter and lard with your fingers in a large bowl until the mixture resembles breadcrumbs. Then add the egg yolks and knead into a ball. Cover with plastic film and chill overnight.

Drain the meat and mix it with the diced bacon, onion, pickled lemon, chopped parsley, salt and pepper. Roll out 1/2 of the dough and line a pie tin, pouring in the mixture. The cover with the rest of the rolled-out dough. Make an opening in the centre and place the pie tin in a warm pre-heated oven (200° C) for one hour after brushing the top with the egg yolk. Meanwhile, prepare a sauce by slowly melting the butter with the flour in a saucepan. Let it brown for several minutes. Pour in the bouillon, bring to the boil; add the vinegar, Madera wine and pepper. Simmer for 10 minutes and serve in a sauce dish.

Note: For a shortcut, you can use pre-prepared sheets of puff or short pastry.

Ombles chevaliers (char), feras, lavarets and trout are excellent fish that can be found in the lakes and streams of the Savoy region. There are many tantalising ways to prepare them. Here are a few of the easiest ones

Fish

Lake Annecy

Ferat fillets

in creamy mushroom sauce

Serves 4 persons

. 1 or 2 fillets per person
. 100 g of butter
. 3 shallots
. 2 cups of dry white wine
. 250 g of button mushrooms
. 100 g of liquid fresh cream
. salt and pepper

Place the fish fillets on a bed of chopped shallots in a well-greased ovenproof dish. Add salt and pepper and the white wine. Cover with buttered greaseproof paper and bake in a moderate oven (180 to 200° C) for 15 minutes or until the fish flakes easily when tested with a fork.

Sauté the mushrooms in butter with some chopped shallots and parsley. Set aside in a warm place. Remove the fish from the oven and drain the stock from the dish. Arrange the fillets on a warm serving platter and garnish with the mushrooms. For the sauce, melt the butter in a saucepan, stir in the flour and gradually add the fish stock as the sauce thickens. Add the cream and continue cooking for a few minutes. Spoon the sauce over the fish just before serving.

Char

This is an excellent freshwater fish that does not require complicated preparation. Here are two very simple recipes for preparing it.

Poached:

Prepare a highly seasoned court-bouillon with parsley,, a shallot, thyme, bay leaf, onion and two cups of good white wine (Crépy, for example) with some water in a shallow pan gently bringing it to the boil. Add the fish and cook (just 15 minutes are necessary for a 600 to 700 g of fish). Carefully lift the fish out. Drain well and serve with melted salted butter and lemon wedges.

Baked:

Sprinkle a buttered ovenproof dish with chopped shallots and parsley. Fill the fish with chopped herbs, salt and pepper and place it in the dish.

Pour some olive oil or fresh cream and two cups of dry white wine over the fish and bake in a moderate oven (180° C) for half an hour.

Chambéry
trout

Serves 6 persons

- 6 trout
- 6 carrots, 6 tomatoes, diced
- 2 onions (one of which stuck with a clove)
- 5 garlic cloves, thyme, bay leaf
- 120 g of fresh cream or butter
- 4 cups of Crépy wine or another dry white wine
- 2 cups of Vermouth (from Chambéry)
- salt and pepper

In a heavy saucepan, prepare a court bouillon with the wine, Vermouth, diced vegetables, aromatic herbs, salt and pepper and some water and bring to a gentle boil for 20 minutes. Then add the trout. Simmer for about 15 minutes.

Carefully lift the fish out and arrange on a heated serving platter with the drained vegetables.

Reduce the fish broth and strain.

Melt butter in a clean saucepan over low heat and stir in flour. Gradually stir in the warm broth and continue stirring until the mixture boils and thickens. Spoon this sauce over the fish and serve warm.

Lavaret quenelles

Lavaret can be prepared in the same way as the féra or the char (omble chevalier). Also, why don't you try to make some delicious homemade quenelles?

Serves 6 persons

. 300 g of lavaret fillets
. 200 g of butter
. 50 g of flour
. 1/4 quart of milk
. 3 eggs
. fish stock

Melt 50 g of butter in a saucepan over low heat, stirring in the flour and cook a few seconds until golden. Add the milk and stir with a wooden spoon until the sauce boils and thickens. This will give you a very thick béchamel sauce. Let it cool.

Meanwhile, mix the fish with the softened butter. Combine these two mixtures and season with salt, pepper and coriander. Work in the egg yolks. Beat the egg whites until soft peaks form and carefully add this to the mixture. Cool for three hours.

Shape the quenelles with the help of two tablespoons and poach them in simmering fish stock for about 10 minutes.

When the quenelles begin to float, carefully remove them and drain. Arrange in an ovenproof dish. Mix together 250 g of liquid cream, 250 g of crushed tomatoes and one tin of lobster bisque. Spoon this over the quenelles and bake in a hot oven for 15 minutes. Serve as soon as they have risen.

Cheeses

Tomme de Savoie

This is one of the oldest cheeses of the region. Once the cream had been separated from the milk and churned into butter, each family used the make Tommes with the remaining low-fat milk and some full-cream milk that had not been used to make butter. It was one of the main dishes at many meals and sometimes the sole source of protein. Tomme has a soft consistency that has been pressed but not cooked. Its grey rind is often sprinkled with orange-coloured mould spots, giving it a rusted look. Today, this cheese can be found in every village market as well as in every large supermarket.

Sérac

This is a fresh, low-fat cheese that is made by curdling a mixture of whey and skim milk. It has given its name to the fields of enormous and threatening ice large blocks that form at the end of most glaciers.

Reblochon

This cheese is made in the Aravis region. Its name comes from the old regional dialect word "reblocher" or "to dodge". In order to reduce the rent that had to be paid to the owner of the cattle and pasture, shepherds did not completely milk their cows. Once the man sent to collect the rent had left, they used to make a delicious cheese with the remaining and much creamier milk. This cheese is made from raw milk and is 14 cm in diameter and 3.5 cm thick. Its production requires 5 quarts of good creamy mountain milk for every cheese and four weeks for drying and curing. It has pinkish to orangey rind. Its texture is creamy and soft. It is just delicious! Once in Thones, the centre of its production, I heard that it was a cheese that "it did not cross the road"; a way of saying that it is best eaten where it is produced.

Beaufort

Several families migrated from the Swiss Gruyere region to the Chablais and Aravis regions to farm the vast pastoral estates of the large Aulps and Reposoir monasteries. They brought with them the method of making Gruyere with milk and rennet cooked in large copper cauldrons. The cheese mixture is then drained, pressed and left to dry for six months. Beaufort cheese is a type of Gruyere made with the very fatty milk produced in the rich Beaufortin pastures. It can also be found in the Haute Maurienne and the Haute Tarentaise. This large round cheese measures 60 centimetres in diameter and is 13 centimetres thick. It has a brownish crust and the cheese is firm, without holes, and has a slight taste of hazelnuts. It is an exceptional cheese.

Abondance

This cheese recalls both the Tomme de Savoie and the Beaufort. It is made with milk from the Abondance Valley. The milk is heated to only 45° C. This cheese is much smaller that the Beaufort, the taste varies from one cheese wheel to another: sometimes very fruity, sometimes very mild. Personally, I find it a very delicious and unusual cheese.

Vacherin

This extremely creamy cheese from Vacheresse is sold wrapped in pine bark. It is rare although it can also be found in the Bauges region, near Aillon-le-Jeune.

Bleu de Temignon

This is a rare blue cheese made from both cow and goat milk, to which a special ferment is added.

Chevrotin

This is a delectable goat cheese, mainly from the Aravis region, that is made using the same technique as the Reblochon cheese. It has a subtle and delicate flavour and a pinkish rind. It is found mainly in the Aravis.

Raclette
and tartiflette

Raclette

This traditional Swiss recipe involved holding the edge of half a raclette cheese in front of the fire in the open fireplace. When the top layer turned golden and melted, it was scraped off (or raclé in French) onto a guest's plate.
One can now buy appliances to heat individual portions of cheese and tip them on one's plate when melted. The melted cheese is best served with boiled potatoes, cured ham and plenty of small pickled onions.
Allow 150 g of raclette cheese and three potatoes per person.

Tartiflette

Please refer to the recipe for "Pela" on page 37.

Reblochon pie

A creamy Reblochon cheese baked in a puff pastry crust. It is easy to make and just delicious!

Serves 4 persons

- 2 sheets of ready-rolled puff pastry
- 1 whole Reblochon cheese
- 1 beaten egg
- 8 slices of local smoked ham

Heat the oven to 220° C.

Spread the pastry on a buttered and floured baking tin forming a circle large enough to wrap around the cheese. Lightly scrape the Reblochon and place it on the pastry dough. Brush the cheese with the beaten egg and cover with the remaining sheet of pastry dough. Seal the edges, trimming away the excess dough.

Brush with the rest of the beaten egg, lower the temperature and bake in a moderate oven (180° C) for about 30 minutes.

Serve hot with a green salad and thin slices of smoked ham.

The fountain at Chinaillon

Talmouses
with Beaufort cheese

Make them as a hot appetizer to be enjoyed with a glass of Savoy white wine. This dish also goes well before a light main course such as fish

Serves 6 persons

- 250 g of puff pastry
- 1/2 quart of milk
- 150 g of flour
- 8 eggs
- 150 g of butter
- 500 g of thinly sliced Beaufort cheese

Melt the butter in a heavy saucepan and add the flour stirring constantly over moderate heat with a wooden spoon. Slowly pour in the milk, bring to the boil, then cook for another two minutes or until the mixture is smooth and thick.

Remove from the heat and whisk the eggs in one by one. Fold in the Beaufort cheese and adjust seasoning to taste.

Cut the sheets of puff pastry and line 12 buttered small tart tins. Place a tablespoon of mixture in the centre of each tin, and bake in a pre-heated moderate oven (200° C) for 25 minutes or until the talmouses are puffed and golden.

Beaufort bridge

Beaufort and Reblochon soufflé

Serves 6 persons

. 50 g of butter
. 50 g of flour
. 1/2 quart of milk
. 5 eggs
. 150 g of Beaufort cheese
. half a Reblochon cheese
. salt, pepper, nutmeg

Grate the Beaufort. Cut the Reblochon into small cubes and put them in the freezer.

Melt the butter in a thick-bottomed pan, and stir in the flour with a wooden spoon. Gradually pour in the milk and bring to a boil. Cook for another five minutes. Season with salt and pepper and add a pinch of nutmeg.

Remove from the heat and cool the mixture a little. Fold in the egg yolks one by one and the grated Beaufort cheese. Beat the egg whites very stiff with a pinch of salt. Heat a moderate oven (200° C).

Butter well a soufflé dish. Blend delicately the egg whites and cubes of frozen Reblochon into the preparation.

Pour this into a greased soufflé dish. Bake in the pre-heated moderate oven for 30 to 40 minutes.

Savoy fondue

A famous Savoy dish which has become popular in many variations, for parties and family meals as well as on the menus in the region's restaurants.

Serves 6

. 400 g of Comté cheese

. 300 g of Beaufort cheese

. 300 g of Emmental cheese

. 125 g of Vacherin cheese
(if in season, otherwise add some more Comté)

. 1 or 2 garlic cloves

. 1 bottle of white wine from Savoy

. half a cup of Kirschwasser

. pepper, nutmeg

Traditionally, the fondue dish (caquelon) is a varnished earthenware pot, although you can use an enamelled pot. On a portable stove, heat six glasses of dry white wine and half a cup of Kirschwasser in an enamelled cast iron pot previously rubbed with garlic with three twists of the pepper mill and a bit of nutmeg. Slowly add the grated cheeses and stir with a wooden spoon until obtaining a smooth and very soft paste. If it is too thick, add some wine.

That's when the fondue is ready. Take the fondue with the portable stove to the dining table.

The guests will have cut small pieces of bread. All that's left is to stick them into the fondue and enjoy.

Berthoud

Per person

- 150 g of Abondance cheese
- _ a cup of Madera wine
  or Savoy white wine
- 1 garlic clove
- pepper, nutmeg

A recipe from the Chablais region; it is small individual fondue prepared with Abondance cheese.

Prepare one ramekin rubbed with garlic for each person. Slice the cheese. Pour in the Madera or white wine. Add pepper and nutmeg.

Put the ramekins in a hot oven for 10 minutes. The Berthoud is best served with bread or on boiled potatoes.

A large chalet at La-Chapelle-d'Abondance

In the mountain regions, desserts used to be rustic, simple and prepared mostly on very special occasions. Oeufs à la neige for weddings and communions, rissoles for Christmas, bugnes for Mardi Gras...

In the small towns, the locals used to cook more refined sweets and pastries, often with chocolate as their main ingredient. All those mouth-watering sweet favourites are still enjoyed today

Desserts

Apple snack

Serves 4 to 6 persons

. 2 eggs
. 125 g of flour
. 4 tablespoons of sugar
. 2 tablespoons of eau de vie
. 2 teaspoons of baking powder
. 4 apples
. 1/2 cup of water

This dessert's name comes from the French "mate faim" or "hunger taming". The local shepherds often used to leave for the day with a sweet or savoury matafan in their pocket.

Mix the beaten eggs with the sugar. Add the eau de vie, flour, baking powder and water until the mixture is smooth. Stir well and add the peeled slices of apples.

Heat a bit of oil in the bottom of a frying pan and pour  the mixture in. Cook it slowly for 30 minutes and then turn the matafan and let it cook for another 15 minutes.

Peasants often went to the fields with a matafan, salted or sprinkled with sugar for their snack.

Sweet épogne

This type of brioche was traditionally baked in the communal oven after the bread.

Dough for 6 persons

. 2 eggs
. 250 g of flour
. 80 g of butter
. 50 g of sugar
. 1 cube active dry yeast
. 1 tablespoon of orange blossom water
. 1 teaspoon of salt

Mix the active dry yeast with a bit of lukewarm water and some flour and set this aside for one hour to rise.

Place the eggs, sugar, orange blossom water, melted butter and flour in a bowl and mix together. Add the yeast mixture and knead the dough for about 15 minutes until it no longer sticks to the fingers. Add a little water if the dough is too dry.

Cover and leave to rise for four hours in a warm place.

Épogne with fruit

Roll the dough out to fit two large buttered tart tins.

Line the pastry shell tightly with fruits (plums, cherries, peaches, raspberries...) and then sprinkle with sugar and bake in a moderate oven (200° C) for 30 minutes.

Savoy gateau

A sweet favourite, this cake is light and airy and delicious served with fruit salad or chocolate mousse. For mouth-watering variations, fill the cooled cake with berries or whipped cream or both or with melted chocolate

Serves 8 persons

- 6 eggs
- 200 g of flour or 150 g of flour and 50 g of cornstarch
- 250 g of sugar
- 1 grated lemon rind

Beat the sugar and egg yolks until obtaining a pale and creamy dough. Sift in the flour and add the cornstarch, lemon zest. Whisk the egg whites until stiff peaks form (1 or 2 drops vinegar and a pinch of salt will help to make the beaten egg whites very stiff). Fold them in carefully in order that they do not fall.

Pour the mixture into a well-buttered round cake tin, and bake in a moderate oven (155° C) for 45 minutes. Check the progress of the cooking with a knife blade.

"Œufs à la neige"

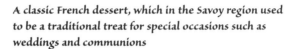

A classic French dessert, which in the Savoy region used to be a traditional treat for special occasions such as weddings and communions

Serves 8 persons

· 1 quart of milk
· 6 eggs
· 150 g of sugar
· 1 vanilla bean

Heat the milk with the vanilla bean to just below boiling point. Meanwhile, beat the egg yolks and sugar in a bowl. In another bowl, whisk the egg whites until stiff peaks form (do not add salt).

Spoon portions of egg whites into the hot milk and cook for one minute on both sides. Drain and set aside in a serving bowl.

Pour the rest of the hot milk into the egg yolk and sugar mixture and beat thoroughly. Return to the saucepan and continue beating over very low heat until the custard thickens. (The cream should not boil.)

Pour the custard on the egg whites.

Prepare a light caramel with 100 g of sugar and pour this over the egg whites just before serving.

Bugnes

Savoy's bakeries sell bugnes at Mardi Gras.
There are several recipes to make this dessert.
This is an easy and light one.

Makes 15 bugnes

- 1 egg
- 1 tablespoon of sugar
- 1 tablespoon of rum
- 1 tablespoon of cooking oil
- 1 pinch of salt
- 6 tablespoons of flour

Beat together the egg, sugar, oil, rum and salt.

Place the flour in a large bowl, make a hole in the centre and pour in the mixture. Knead the dough well until it feels smooth and elastic when pressed, and then roll out the dough with a rolling pin as thin as possible. The thinner the bugnes, the quicker they will cook. Cut the dough into elongated rectangles, making a slit in the middle in order to be able to stick one end of the rectangle through this slit.

Heat some cooking oil in a saucepan over medium-low heat.

Cook the bugnes in the boiling oil until golden and puffed.

Drain on a paper towel and sprinkle with icing sugar.

Pear rissoles

Rissoles used to be prepared at Christmas following a time-consuming recipe with the cook having to prepare both the puff pastry and the pear compote. Nowadays, it is significantly easier to use sheets of puff pastry that are readily available in most supermarkets.

Makes 12 to 15 rissoles

- 250 g of flour
- 150 g of butter
- 2 kg of pears
- 400 g of sugar
- 1 pinch of salt
- 1 pinch of cinnamon
- 1 pinch of ginger
- 2 sheets of puff pastry dough

Use the flaky pastry dough or make a short dough with the flour, very cold butter cut into strips, a pinch of salt, one tablespoon of sugar and a bit of cold water.

Roll out the dough as thinly as possible. Cut out round pieces of dough with a large bowl. Place a portion of thick compote on them—made with peeled pears, sugar and spices—after cooking for a long time in order to dry out the compote.

Fold over the circle of dough and then seal the edges by pressing with your thumb. Place the rissoles on a buttered tin lined with non-stick baking paper and cook them in a moderate oven (200° C) for 15 to 20 minutes.

Sabayon

Serves 4 persons

. 1/4 quart of sparkling or dry white wine
. 5 egg yolks
. 4 chopped mint leaves
. 1 or 2 drops of vanilla extract
. 1100 g of sugar

This is an intriguing, light and fluffy dessert prepared with sparkling Savoy wine or even Champagne, egg yolks and sugar. It can be served in individual glasses with fresh berries or a Savoy gateau or almond biscuits.

Beat the egg yolks and sugar into a mixing bowl until well combined. Pour the mixture into a heavy saucepan, add the wine, mint and vanilla extract and cook over low heat, stirring constantly until the mixture is thick and frothy.

Keep the saucepan warm in a double boiler until just before serving.

To make an enticing hot fruit pudding, place strawberries, raspberries, bananas and blackberries in an ovenproof dish and spoon on the sabayon. Place under a pre-heated hot grill and cook for two to three minutes or until the top is golden.

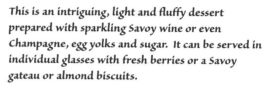

An apple pie
from Salins-les-Bains

Serves 6 to 8 persons

. 300 g of flour
. 150 g of butter, softened
  1 egg
. 200 g of sugar
. 1 package (or 4 teaspoons) of yeast
. 1 lemon
. 100 g of crushed hazelnuts
. 3 apples
. 100 g of sultanas
. 100 g of chopped candied fruits
. 4 tablespoons of rum

Delicious, but you have to begin early in order to give the dough time to rise

Soak the sultanas in the heated rum for three hours. Mix the flour, butter, egg, sugar, yeast and the zest of half a lemon. Knead the dough and let it rest for three to four hours at room temperature.

Heat the rum-sultana mixture and then remove it from the stove and flambé it. Add the chopped candied fruits, the zest of the other half of the lemon, the peeled and thinly sliced apples, the crushed hazelnuts and four tablespoons of sugar. Roll out the dough and fit half of it into a buttered and lightly floured tart tin. Pour in the fruit mixture and cover with the remaining dough. Seal the edges and glaze with a little milk and cream.

Bake in a moderate oven for at least 30 minutes. The cake should rise and be well browned.

Chocolate truffles

Chocolate truffles were created in Chambery by a confectioner, M. Dufour, one December day in 1815 when he found himself short of chocolate sweets to sell. He had the brilliant idea of mixing dark chocolate with fresh cream and a bit of vanilla. This is his recipe for about 2 lbs of truffles

Makes 80 to 100 truffles

For the truffles:

. 750 g of good-quality dark or semi-bitter semi-bitter chocolate
. 500 g of fresh cream
. icing sugar

For the coating:

. unsweetened cocoa
. 350 g of dark cooking chocolate

Melt the chocolate in a double boiler. When it has melted, add the fresh cream and let simmer for another two to three minutes.

Stir until the mixture is smooth and creamy. Pour this into a bowl and refrigerate for at least 12 hours. Make small truffles with your fingers and roll them quickly in icing sugar. Place them in the freezer for four to six hours.

Grate the cooking chocolate for the coating onto a baking tray and heat in a very low oven.

Roll the frozen truffles in the melted chocolate and then dip them one by one in a bowl of cocoa. Refrigerate them overnight to harden.

Note: The truffles can be perfumed with vanilla, coffee, rum, cognac...

Traditional *chocolate mousse*

Serves 4 persons

- 3 eggs
- 125 g of good-quality dark chocolate
- 100 g of butter
- no sugar

Melt the chocolate slowly in a double boiler. When it has melted, add the butter cut into pieces, mix well and let cool. Then add the egg yolks and stir until the mixture is smooth.

Whisk the egg whites until stiff. Pour the chocolate mixture over the stiff egg whites and fold in carefully. Pour this into a serving bowl and refrigerate for at least three hours.

Note: The butter can be replaced by whipped fresh cream. The mousse will be fluffier but just as delicious.

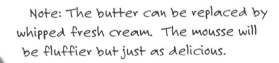

Gentian wine

The mountain villagers in Savoy are quite often adept at preparing liqueurs and wines from gentian. Here is a recipe for gentian wine

- 6 bottles of not-too-dry white wine
- 150 g of gentian roots, peeled and sliced
- the grated rind from two non-treated oranges
- 1.25 kg of sugar
- 6 cups of eau de vie

Place all the ingredients in a demijohn and let the mixture macerate for four days. Strain and pour into bottles.

Mulled wine

- 1 bottle of red wine
- 125 g of sugar
- 1 orange
- 1 clove
- ginger and cinnamon

Heat the sugar, red wine, clove, ginger and cinnamon in a saucepan and stir until the sugar has dissolved. Add the juice of the orange, and then simmer gently for another minute. Then serve.

Mulled wine

with a Savoy twist

- 1 bottle of red wine
- 125 g of sugar
- 1 lemon
- 1 clove
- 1 bay leaf
- 1 sprig of thyme

Put the sugar and red wine in a saucepan, bring to the boil and stir until the sugar has dissolved. Add the spices and the lemon cut into thin slices.

Simmer for another minute. Remove from the heat, flambé the wine for one or two minutes and serve.

Contents

Soups — 4

Milk and flour soup 6
Pasta soup 7
Soup with greens 8
Nettle soup 9
Onion soup 10
Sorrel soup 11
A hearty soup 12
Pumpkin soup 13
Chestnut soup 14
Wild garlic soup 15

Salads and vegetables — 16

Potato salad 18
Dandelion salad 19
Spinach omelette 20
Spinach bread 21
Swiss chard gratin 21
Baked cabbage parcels 22
Cardoon gratin 23
Cabbage with chestnuts 24
Savoyard leeks 26
Mange-tout or sweet peas 27
Turnips 28
Buttered turnips 29
Turnips gratin 29
Salted épogne 30
Epogne with vegetables 31
Carrots Val de Thônes 32
Pumpkin gratin 33

Potatoes, polenta and pasta — 34

"Fricassée" 36
"Fricassée" with Reblochon cheese 37
"Paillasson" potatoes 38

"Ravioles" from the Chablais region 39
Scalloped potatoes 40
"Farcon" from Faucigny 41
"Farcement" 42
Cabbage farcement 43
Polenta 44
Polenta gnocchi 46
Deep fried polenta 46
Polenta farcement 47
Crozets 48
Home-made crozets 48
Ready-to-cook crozets 48
Cooking "fides" style 49

Meat — 50

Diots in white wine 52
Beaufort Diots 52
Other sausages and how to cook them 53
Potée savoyarde 54
Stuffed cabbage 55
Attriaux and Fricassée 56
Pork paupiettes with Reblochon cheese 57
Pork casserole with red wine and cream 58
Braised veal with fresh cream 59
Braised beef with white wine
and mushroom sauce 60
Chambéry Beef Aiguillette 61
Pullet with Beaufort cheese 62
Chambéry veal paté 63

Fish — 64

Ferat fillets in creamy mushroom sauce 66
Char 67

Chambéry trout 68
Lavaret quenelles 69

Cheeses — 70

Few words about cheeses 72
Raclette and tartiflette 74
Reblochon pie 75
Talmouses with Beaufort cheese 76
Beaufort and Reblochon soufflé 77
Savoy fondue 78
Berthoud 79

Desserts — 80

Apple snack 82
Sweet épogne 83
Epogne with fruit 83
Savoy gâteau 84
"Œufs à la neige" 85
Bugnes 86
Pear rissoles 87
Sabayon 88
An apple pie from Salins-les-Bains 89
Chocolate truffles 90
Traditional chocolate mousse 91
Gentian wine 92
Mulled wine 93
Mulled wine with a Savoy twist 93

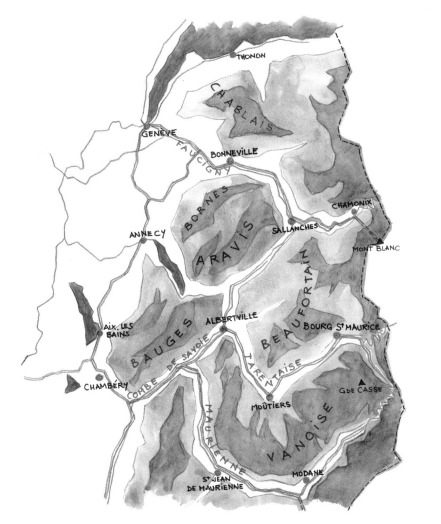

THONON

CHABLAIS

GENÈVE

FAUCIGNY

BONNEVILLE

CHAMONIX

BORNES

SALLANCHES

ANNECY

ARAVIS

MONT BLANC

BEAUFORTAIN

AIX. LES BAINS

BAUGES

ALBERTVILLE

BOURG St MAURICE

COMBE DE SAVOIE

TARENTAISE

CHAMBÉRY

MAURIENNE

MOÛTIERS

G DE CASSE

VANOISE

St JEAN DE MAURIENNE

MODANE

Printed in Europe